Disclaimer

The SQL coding challenges and solutions presented in this book are intended solely for educational and practice purposes. While some of the problems may be inspired by or similar to those found on coding platforms like LeetCode or in the technical interview processes of FAANG companies (Facebook, Amazon, Apple, Netflix, and Google), the content in this book has been curated, modified, and presented independently by the author.

The author does not claim ownership or affiliation with any specific coding platform, company, or interview process. The challenges and solutions are provided as original works of the author, based on their research, experience, and understanding of SQL and database concepts.

Any resemblance to actual coding challenges or interview questions from FAANG companies, LeetCode, or other sources is unintentional and should not be construed as a violation of intellectual property rights or confidentiality agreements.

This book and its content are intended for personal use and educational purposes only. They should not be used for commercial purposes, distributed, or reproduced without the express written consent of the author and publisher.

The author and publisher shall not be held liable for any direct, indirect, incidental, or consequential damages arising from the use of this book or its content, including but not limited to any alleged violations of intellectual property rights, confidentiality breaches, or any other legal issues.

Readers are advised to use this book and its content responsibly, respecting the intellectual property rights of coding platforms, companies, and other entities. The author and publisher strongly condemn any unauthorized use or distribution of copyrighted material.

By reading or using this book, you acknowledge and agree to the terms of this disclaimer and understand the independent and educational nature of the content provided herein.

Table of Contents

Disclaimer *1*

Table of Contents *2*

1. *Human Traffic of Stadiums*.................................*6*

2. *Game Play Analysis II*.......................................*7*

3. *Game Play Analysis III*......................................*8*

4. *Game Play Analysis IV*......................................*9*

5. *Game Play Analysis V*.....................................*10*

6. *Department Top Three Salaries*.......................*11*

7. *Project Employees II*..*13*

8. *Capital Gain/Loss*..*14*

9. *Trips and Users* *15*

10. *Friendly Movies Streamed Last Month* *16*

11. *New Users Daily Count* *17*

12. *Product Sales Analysis I*.................................*18*

13. *Product Sales Analysis II*................................*19*

14. *Product Sales Analysis III* *20*

16. *Monthly Transactions I*...................................*21*

17. *Monthly Transactions II*..................................*22*

18. *Bank Account Summary* *23*

19. *Bank Account Summary II*...............................*24*

20. *Student Course Enrollment*.............................*25*

21. Apples & Oranges 26

22. Sales by Date 27

23. Customer Placing the Largest Number of Orders 28

24. Shortest Distance in a Plane 29

25. Movie Rating 30

26. Contest Leaderboard 31

27. Student Contest Rank 32

28. Flights from City A to City B 33

29. Duplicate Records 34

30. Biggest Window 35

31. Friend Requests I 36

32. Friend Requests II 37

33. Investment Bank 38

34. Top 3 Revenue Products 39

35. New User Follows.........................40

36. Consecutive Available Seats 41

37. Employees With Missing Information............42

38. Rank Scores................................43

39. Find Follower Counts....................44

40. Tournament Winners 45

41. Managers with at Least 5 Direct Reports........46

42. Find Followers Count 47

43. Find Cumulative Salary of an Employee 48

44. Nth Highest Salary 49

45. Department Highest Salary 50

46. Duplicate Emails..51

47. Fixed Point 52

48. Consecutive Numbers 53

49. Rising Temperature 54

50. Delete Duplicate Emails................................55

51. Sales Person 56

52. Find Customer Referee 57

53. Customer Who Visited but Did Not Make Any Transactions..58

54. Second Highest Salary 59

55. Percentage of Repeated Players 60

56. Total Sales Amount by Year...........................61

57. User Purchase Platform................................62

58. Product Price at a Given Date........................63

59. Task Scheduler 64

60. Biggest Single Number 65

61. Customers Who Never Order 66

62. Investments in 2016 67

63.   *Swap Salary* *68*

1. Human Traffic of Stadiums

Question: Write an SQL query to display the stadium and the total number of people visiting it after each match ordered by the number of people in descending order.

```
Stadium (id, visit_date, people)
```

Solution:

```sql
SELECT
    s.id,
    s.visit_date,
    s.people
FROM
    (SELECT
        id,
        visit_date,
        SUM(people) OVER (PARTITION BY id ORDER BY visit_date) AS people
    FROM
        Stadium) s
GROUP BY s.id, s.visit_date, s.people
ORDER BY s.people DESC;
```

2. Game Play Analysis II

Question: Write an SQL query to report the `device` that is first logged in for each player.

Activity (player_id, device_id, event_date, games_played)

Solution:

```sql
SELECT
    player_id,
    device_id
FROM
    (SELECT
        player_id,
        device_id,
        RANK() OVER (PARTITION BY player_id ORDER BY event_date)
AS rank
    FROM
        Activity) ranked
WHERE
    ranked.rank = 1;
```

3. Game Play Analysis III

Question: Write an SQL query to report the first login date for each player.

Activity (player_id, device_id, event_date, games_played)

Solution:

```sql
SELECT
    player_id,
    MIN(event_date) AS first_login
FROM
    Activity
GROUP BY
    player_id;
```

4. Game Play Analysis IV

Question: Write an SQL query to find the fraction of players that logged in again on the day after the day they first logged in, rounded to 2 decimal places. In other words, you need to find the fraction of player_ids that logged in for at least two consecutive days starting from their first login date.

Activity (player_id, device_id, event_date, games_played)

Solution:

```
SELECT
  ROUND(
    COUNT(DISTINCT player_id) * 1.0
    / (SELECT COUNT(DISTINCT player_id) FROM Activity), 2
  ) AS fraction
FROM
  (SELECT
    player_id,
    EVENT_DATE,
    LEAD(EVENT_DATE, 1) OVER (PARTITION BY player_id
ORDER BY EVENT_DATE) AS next_date
  FROM
    Activity) t
WHERE
  DATEDIFF(next_date, EVENT_DATE) = 1;
```

5. Game Play Analysis V

Question: Write an SQL query to report the first login date, last login date, and the number of logins for each player.

Activity (player_id, device_id, event_date, games_played)

Solution:

```sql
SELECT
    player_id,
    MIN(event_date) AS first_login,
    MAX(event_date) AS last_login,
    COUNT(*) AS login_count
FROM
    Activity
GROUP BY
    player_id;
```

6. Department Top Three Salaries

Question: Write a SQL query to find employees who earn the top three salaries in each department. For the above tables, a top three salary query should generate the following table:

```
Employee (id, name, salary, departmentId)
Department (id, name)
```

Solution:

```sql
SELECT
    d.name AS 'Department',
    e.name AS 'Employee',
    e.salary
FROM
    Employee e
JOIN
    Department d ON e.departmentId = d.id
WHERE
    (e.departmentId, e.salary) IN (
        SELECT
            departmentId,
            salary
        FROM
            (SELECT
                departmentId,
                salary,
                DENSE_RANK() OVER (PARTITION BY departmentId
ORDER BY salary DESC) AS 'rank'
```

```sql
    FROM
        Employee) ranked
    WHERE
        ranked.rank <= 3
)
ORDER BY
    d.name,
    e.salary DESC;
```

7. Project Employees II

Question: Write an SQL query that reports the `project_id` and the total number of `experienced` employees there are for that `project`, where `experienced` employees are `Employees` with at least three years of experience.

```
Project (project_id, employee_id)
Employee (employee_id, name, experience_years)
```

Solution:

```sql
SELECT
    p.project_id,
    COUNT(e.employee_id) AS experienced_employees
FROM
    Project p
JOIN
    Employee e ON p.employee_id = e.employee_id
WHERE
    e.experience_years >= 3
GROUP BY
    p.project_id;
```

8. Capital Gain/Loss

Question: Write an SQL query to report the capital gain/loss for each stock.

The rules are:

- Buy `operation_day` is smaller than `sell` `operation_day`.
- The `Capital gain/loss` of each stock is the sum of `sell_price` - `buy_price` for every stock.

Stocks (stock_name, operation, operation_day, price)

Solution:

```
SELECT
    stock_name,
    SUM(
        CASE
            WHEN operation = 'Buy' THEN -price
            ELSE price
        END
    ) AS capital_gain_loss
FROM
    Stocks
GROUP BY
    stock_name;
```

9. Trips and Users

Question: Write a SQL query to find the cancellation rate of requests with unbanned users (both client and driver) in each city. For the above tables, the cancellation rate is calculated as follows:

Rate = Number of Cancelled (by client or driver) / Total Number of Requests

Trips (Id, Client_Id, Driver_Id, City_Id, Status, Request_at)

Users (Users_Id, Banned, Role)

Solution:

```sql
SELECT
  t.City_Id,
  ROUND(
    SUM(CASE WHEN t.Status LIKE 'cancelled_%' THEN 1 ELSE 0
END) * 1.0
    / COUNT(t.Id),
    2
  ) AS 'Cancellation Rate'
FROM Trips t
JOIN Users c ON t.Client_Id = c.Users_Id
JOIN Users d ON t.Driver_Id = d.Users_Id
WHERE c.Banned = 'No'
  AND d.Banned = 'No'
GROUP BY t.City_Id;
```

10. Friendly Movies Streamed Last Month

Question: Write an SQL query to report the distinct titles of the movies streamed by the user 'Winston' last month. Here's the schema:

```
ActivityLog (user_id, session_id, activity_type, activity_date)
Movies (movie_id, title, genres)
```

Solution:

```
SELECT
    m.title
FROM
    ActivityLog a
JOIN
    Movies m ON a.activity_type = CONCAT('stream,', m.movie_id)
WHERE
    a.user_id = (SELECT user_id FROM ActivityLog WHERE user_id =
'Winston' LIMIT 1)
    AND a.activity_date BETWEEN '2023-02-01' AND '2023-02-28'
GROUP BY
    m.title;
```

11. New Users Daily Count

Question: Write an SQL query to calculate the number of new users for each day.

```
Traffic (user_id, activity, entry_time)
```

Solution:

```sql
SELECT
    entry_time AS login_date,
    COUNT(DISTINCT user_id) AS new_users
FROM
    Traffic
WHERE
    activity = 'login'
GROUP BY
    login_date;
```

12. Product Sales Analysis I

Question: Write an SQL query to find for each product, the product_name and the total amount of sales in the period 2019 for each product.

Product (product_id, product_name)

Sales (product_id, period_name, sales_amount)

Solution:

```
SELECT
    p.product_name,
    SUM(s.sales_amount) AS total_amount
FROM
    Product p
JOIN
    Sales s ON p.product_id = s.product_id
WHERE
    s.period_name LIKE '2019%'
GROUP BY
    p.product_name;
```

13. Product Sales Analysis II

Question: Write an SQL query to report the total revenue of each product for each year, sorted by ascending order of the product ID.

```
Product (product_id, product_name)
Sales (product_id, sale_year, sale_amount)
```

Solution:

```sql
SELECT
    p.product_id,
    p.product_name,
    s.sale_year,
    SUM(s.sale_amount) AS total_revenue
FROM
    Product p
LEFT JOIN
    Sales s ON p.product_id = s.product_id
GROUP BY
    p.product_id, p.product_name, s.sale_year
ORDER BY
    p.product_id, s.sale_year;
```

14. Product Sales Analysis III

Question: Write an SQL query to get the product_id and the year that had the maximum revenue.

Sales (product_id, sale_year, sale_amount)

Solution:

```sql
SELECT
    product_id,
    sale_year
FROM
    Sales
GROUP BY
    product_id, sale_year
ORDER BY
    product_id, SUM(sale_amount) DESC;
```

16. Monthly Transactions I

Question: Write an SQL query to find the number of transactions in each country and state for each month.

Transactions (trans_id, country, state, amount, trans_date)

Solution:

```sql
SELECT
    DATE_FORMAT(trans_date, '%Y-%m') AS month,
    country,
    state,
    COUNT(*) AS num_transactions
FROM
    Transactions
GROUP BY
    month, country, state;
```

17.Monthly Transactions II

Question: Write an SQL query to report the total revenue, total number of transactions, and the number of approved transactions for each month.

Transactions (trans_id, country, state, amount, trans_date, approved)

Solution:

```
SELECT
    DATE_FORMAT(trans_date, '%Y-%m') AS month,
    SUM(amount) AS total_revenue,
    COUNT(*) AS total_transactions,
    SUM(CASE WHEN approved = 'Y' THEN 1 ELSE 0 END) AS
approved_transactions
FROM
    Transactions
GROUP BY
    month;
```

18. Bank Account Summary

Question: Write an SQL query to get the total sum of the amount from the Transactions table, grouped by the user_id and the transaction_type.

```
Transactions (transaction_id, user_id, transaction_type, amount, transaction_date)
```

Solution:

```sql
SELECT
    user_id,
    transaction_type,
    SUM(amount) AS total_amount
FROM
    Transactions
GROUP BY
    user_id, transaction_type;
```

19. Bank Account Summary II

Question: Write an SQL query to get the total capital deposited at each bank, and the number of users who deposited and withdrew money for each bank.

```
Users (user_id, user_name)
Transactions (trans_id, bank_id, amount, trans_type)
```

Solution:

```sql
SELECT
    t.bank_id,
    SUM(CASE WHEN t.trans_type = 'Deposit' THEN t.amount ELSE 0
END) AS total_deposit,
    COUNT(DISTINCT CASE WHEN t.trans_type = 'Deposit' THEN
u.user_id END) AS depositors,
    COUNT(DISTINCT CASE WHEN t.trans_type = 'Withdraw' THEN
u.user_id END) AS withdrawers
FROM
    Transactions t
JOIN
    Users u ON t.bank_id = u.user_id
GROUP BY
    t.bank_id;
```

20. Student Course Enrollment

Question: Write a SQL query to get the total number of students enrolled in each course.

```
Courses (course_id, course_name)
```

```
Student (student_id, student_name)
Enrollment (student_id, course_id)
```

Solution:

```sql
SELECT
  c.course_name,
  COUNT(e.student_id) AS student_count
FROM
  Courses c
LEFT JOIN
  Enrollment e ON c.course_id = e.course_id
GROUP BY
  c.course_name;
```

21. Apples & Oranges

Question: Write an SQL query to find the number of apples and oranges in each box.

Boxes (box_id, apple_count, orange_count)

Solution:

```sql
SELECT
    box_id,
    apple_count,
    orange_count
FROM
    Boxes
WHERE
    apple_count >= 1 OR orange_count >= 1;
```

22.Sales by Date

Question: Write an SQL query to calculate the total revenue generated from each `product` on each date.

```
Orders (order_date, paid_date, invoice)
Company (sale_id, product_id, product_name, product_category,
product_price)
```

Solution:

```sql
SELECT
    o.order_date,
    SUM(c.product_price) AS total_revenue
FROM
    Orders o
JOIN
    Company c ON o.invoice = c.sale_id
WHERE
    o.paid_date IS NOT NULL
GROUP BY
    o.order_date
ORDER BY
    o.order_date;
```

23.Customer Placing the Largest Number of Orders

Question: Write an SQL query to find the customer who has placed the largest number of orders.

Orders (order_id, customer_id)

Solution:

```sql
SELECT
    customer_id
FROM
    Orders
GROUP BY
    customer_id
ORDER BY
    COUNT(order_id) DESC
LIMIT 1;
```

24. Shortest Distance in a Plane

Question: Write an SQL query to find the shortest distance between two points in the `Point2D` table.

Point2D (x, y)

Solution:

```sql
SELECT
  ROUND(
    SQRT(
      MIN(
        POW(p1.x - p2.x, 2) + POW(p1.y - p2.y, 2)
      )
    ),
    2
  ) AS shortest
FROM
  Point2D p1
JOIN
  Point2D p2 ON p1.x <> p2.x OR p1.y <> p2.y;
```

25.Movie Rating

Question: Write an SQL query to select the movie with the highest rating. If there is a tie, select the movie with the larger number of votes.

Movies (movie_id, title, avg_rating, total_votes)

Solution:

```sql
SELECT
    title
FROM
    Movies
WHERE
    (avg_rating, total_votes) = (
        SELECT
            MAX(avg_rating), MAX(total_votes)
        FROM
            Movies
    )
LIMIT 1;
```

26.Contest Leaderboard

Question: Write an SQL query to find the winner in each contest. The winner is the user who scored the highest rating in the contest. If there is a tie, the user with the smaller `user_id` wins.

```
Users (user_id, name)
Contests (contest_id, gold_medal, silver_medal, kicked)
Views (user_id, contest_id, rating)
```

Solution:

```sql
SELECT
    contest_id,
    user_id AS winner
FROM
    (SELECT
        contest_id,
        user_id,
        RANK() OVER (PARTITION BY contest_id ORDER BY rating
DESC, user_id) AS rank
    FROM
        Views) ranked
WHERE
    ranked.rank = 1;
```

27.Student Contest Rank

Question: Write an SQL query to find the `rank` of each student. The `rank` is calculated based on the `student_marks` in descending order. If there are multiple students with the same `student_marks`, they should share the same rank.

Students (student_id, student_name, student_marks)

Solution:

```sql
SELECT
    student_id,
    student_name,
    student_marks,
    DENSE_RANK() OVER (ORDER BY student_marks DESC) AS 'rank'
FROM
    Students;
```

28. Flights from City A to City B

Question: Write an SQL query to find the cheapest price from city A to city B with at most two flights.

Flights (flight_id, from_city, to_city, price)

Solution:

```sql
SELECT
    MIN(f1.price + COALESCE(f2.price, 0)) AS cheapest_price
FROM
    Flights f1
LEFT JOIN
    Flights f2 ON f1.to_city = f2.from_city AND f2.to_city = 'B'
WHERE
    f1.from_city = 'A'
    AND COALESCE(f2.to_city, 'B') = 'B';
```

29.Duplicate Records

Question: Write an SQL query to remove duplicate records from the Employees table.

Employees (id, name, department, salary)

Solution:

```
DELETE e1
FROM
    Employees e1,
    Employees e2
WHERE
    e1.id < e2.id
    AND e1.name = e2.name
    AND e1.department = e2.department
    AND e1.salary = e2.salary;
```

30.Biggest Window

Question: Write an SQL query to find the biggest window in each tree. A window is an interval between the `left_value` and `right_value` of two nodes.

Installation (id, parent_id, left_value, right_value)

Solution:

```
SELECT
    i1.id,
    i1.parent_id,
    i1.left_value,
    i1.right_value,
    MAX(i2.right_value) - MIN(i1.left_value) + 1 AS window
FROM
    Installation i1
JOIN
    Installation i2 ON i1.left_value <= i2.left_value AND i2.right_value <=
i1.right_value
GROUP BY
    i1.id
ORDER BY
    window DESC
LIMIT 1;
```

31.Friend Requests I

Question: Write an SQL query to find the overall percentage of requests that were accepted.

```
FriendRequest (sender_id, send_to_id, request_date)
RequestAccepted (requester_id, accepter_id, accepted_date)
```

Solution:

```sql
SELECT
  ROUND(IFNULL(
    (SELECT COUNT(*) FROM
      (SELECT
        requester_id,
        accepter_id
      FROM RequestAccepted
      UNION ALL
      SELECT
        send_to_id AS requester_id,
        sender_id AS accepter_id
      FROM FriendRequest) t
    ) * 1.0 / (SELECT COUNT(*) FROM FriendRequest),
    0
  ), 2
) AS accept_rate;
```

32.Friend Requests II

Question: Write a SQL query to find the overall percentage of requests that were accepted, rounded to 2 decimal places.

```
FriendRequest (sender_id, send_to_id, request_date)
RequestAccepted (requester_id, accepter_id, accepted_date)
```

Solution:

```sql
SELECT ROUND(IFNULL((SELECT COUNT(*)
        FROM (SELECT
                requester_id,
                accepter_id
            FROM
                RequestAccepted
            UNION ALL
            SELECT
                send_to_id AS requester_id,
                sender_id AS accepter_id
            FROM
                FriendRequest) t
        ) * 1.0 / (SELECT COUNT(*) FROM FriendRequest),
        0
    ), 2
) AS accept_rate;
```

33. Investment Bank

Question: Write an SQL query to find the total investment amount and the number of investors for each investment date.

```
Investments (investment_id, investor_id, amount, date)
InvestorInfo (investor_id, name, age)
```

Solution:

```sql
SELECT
    i.date,
    SUM(i.amount) AS total_investment,
    COUNT(DISTINCT i.investor_id) AS num_investors
FROM
    Investments i
JOIN
    InvestorInfo ii ON i.investor_id = ii.investor_id
GROUP BY
    i.date;
```

34.Top 3 Revenue Products

Question: Write an SQL query to find the top 3 product revenue values in each year and period.

```
Product (product_id, product_name, year, price)
Sales (product_id, period, sales_count)
```

Solution:

```sql
SELECT
    p.product_name,
    p.year,
    p.price * s.sales_count AS revenue,
    s.period
FROM
    Product p
JOIN
    Sales s ON p.product_id = s.product_id
ORDER BY
    p.year,
    s.period,
    revenue DESC
LIMIT 1000;
```

35.New User Follows

Question: Write an SQL query to find the number of new users that followed each contest after the contest started.

Followers (user_id, follower_id)

Contests (contest_id, gold_medal, silver_medal)

Views (user_id, contest_id, rating)

Solution:

```sql
SELECT
    c.contest_id,
    COUNT(f.follower_id) AS new_followers
FROM
    Contests c
CROSS JOIN Followers f
WHERE f.follower_id NOT IN (
    SELECT
        user_id
    FROM
        Views
    WHERE
        contest_id = c.contest_id
    )
GROUP BY
    c.contest_id;
```

36. Consecutive Available Seats

Question: Write an SQL query to find the number of unoccupied seats for each two consecutive rows in the seat table.

Cinema (seat_id, free)

Solution:

```sql
SELECT
    DISTINCT c1.seat_id AS seat_id
FROM
    Cinema c1
JOIN
    Cinema c2 ON ABS(c1.seat_id - c2.seat_id) = 1
    AND c1.free = 1
    AND c2.free = 1
ORDER BY
    c1.seat_id;
```

37. Employees With Missing Information

Question: Write a SQL query to find the employees who have the missing information.

Employees (employee_id, name)

Salaries (employee_id, salary)

Solution:

```sql
SELECT
  e.employee_id
FROM Employees e
WHERE e.employee_id NOT IN
(SELECT employee_id Salaries)
UNION
SELECT s.employee_id FROM Salaries s
WHERE
  s.employee_id NOT IN (
    SELECT
      employee_id
    FROM
      Employees
  )
ORDER BY
  employee_id;
```

38. Rank Scores

Question: Write a SQL query to rank the scores. The ranking should be calculated for each group of scores with the same score. If there is a tie between two scores, both should have the same ranking.

Scores (id, score)

Solution:

```sql
SELECT
    score,
    DENSE_RANK() OVER (ORDER BY score DESC) AS 'rank'
FROM
    Scores
ORDER BY
    score DESC;
```

39. Find Follower Counts

Question: Write a SQL query to get the follower counts of each user.

Followers (user_id, follower_id)

Solution:

```sql
SELECT
    user_id,
    COUNT(DISTINCT follower_id) AS follower_count
FROM
    Followers
GROUP BY
    user_id;
```

40. Tournament Winners

Question: Write a SQL query to find the winner of each tournament group.

```
Players (player_id, group_id)
Matches (match_id, first_player, second_player, first_score, second_score)
```

Solution:

```sql
SELECT p.group_id, p.player_id
FROM Players p
JOIN (SELECT first_player AS player_id,
    SUM(first_score) AS total_score
  FROM Matches
  GROUP BY first_player
  UNION ALL
  SELECT second_player AS player_id,
    SUM(second_score) AS total_score
  FROM Matches
  GROUP BY second_player) m
  ON p.player_id = m.player_id
GROUP BY p.group_id
ORDER BY p.group_id, m.total_score DESC, p.player_id;
```

41. Managers with at Least 5 Direct Reports

Question: Write an SQL query to find the managers with at least 5 direct reports.

```
Employee (id, name, department, managerId)
```

Solution:

```
SELECT
   e1.name
FROM
   Employee e1
JOIN
   (SELECT
      managerId,
      COUNT(*) AS reports
   FROM
      Employee
   GROUP BY
      managerId
   HAVING
      COUNT(*) >= 5) e2
ON e1.id = e2.managerId;
```

42.Find Followers Count

Question: Write an SQL query to find the follower count for each user.

```
Followers (user_id, follower_id)
```

Solution:

```
SELECT
   user_id,
```

```sql
    COUNT(DISTINCT follower_id) AS follower_count
FROM
    Followers
GROUP BY
    user_id;
```

43.Find Cumulative Salary of an Employee

Question: Write an SQL query to find the cumulative salary of each employee over time.

Employee (id, month, salary)

Solution:

```sql
SELECT
    id,
    month,
    SUM(salary) OVER (PARTITION BY id ORDER BY month) AS
cumulative_salary
FROM
    Employee;
```

44. Nth Highest Salary

Question: Write a SQL query to get the nth highest salary from the "Employee" table.

Employee (id, salary)

Solution:

```sql
CREATE FUNCTION getNthHighestSalary(@N INT) RETURNS INT
BEGIN
  RETURN (
    SELECT DISTINCT Salary
    FROM (
      SELECT Salary, DENSE_RANK() OVER (ORDER BY Salary
DESC) AS 'RankDesc'
      FROM Employee
    ) AS RankedSalaries
    WHERE RankDesc = @N
  );
END;
```

45. Department Highest Salary

Question: Write a SQL query to find employees who have the highest salary in each department.

```
Employee (id, name, salary, departmentId)
Department (id, name)
```

Solution:

```sql
SELECT
    d.name AS 'Department',
    e.name AS 'Employee',
    e.salary AS 'Salary'
FROM
    Employee e
JOIN
    Department d ON e.departmentId = d.id
WHERE
    (e.departmentId, e.salary) IN (
        SELECT
            departmentId,
            MAX(salary)
        FROM
            Employee
        GROUP BY departmentId  );
```

46. Duplicate Emails

Question: Write a SQL query to find all duplicate email addresses in a table named "Person".

Person (id, email)

Solution:

```sql
SELECT
    email
FROM
    Person
GROUP BY
    email
HAVING
    COUNT(email) > 1;
```

47.Fixed Point

Question: Write a SQL query to find the fixed point in the given array (where the value is equal to its index).

Numbers (num, val)

Solution:

```sql
SELECT
    num
FROM
    Numbers
WHERE
    num = val;
```

48. Consecutive Numbers

Question: Write a SQL query to find all the consecutive numbers from the "Logs" table.

Logs (id, num)

Solution:

```
SELECT
    DISTINCT l1.num AS ConsecutiveNums
FROM
    Logs l1
JOIN
    Logs l2 ON l1.id = l2.id - 1
JOIN
    Logs l3 ON l1.id = l3.id - 2
WHERE
    l1.num = l2.num
    AND l2.num = l3.num;
```

49. Rising Temperature

Question: Write an SQL query to find all dates' ids with higher temperatures compared to its previous dates (yesterday).

Weather (id, recordDate, temperature)

Solution:

```sql
SELECT
    w2.id
FROM
    Weather w1
JOIN
    Weather w2 ON DATEDIFF(w2.recordDate, w1.recordDate) = 1
WHERE
    w2.temperature > w1.temperature;
```

50.Delete Duplicate Emails

Question: Write a SQL query to delete all duplicate email entries in a table named "Person", keeping only unique emails based on the smallest id.

```
Person (id, email)
```

Solution:

```
DELETE p1
FROM
    Person p1,
    Person p2
WHERE
    p1.email = p2.email
    AND p1.id > p2.id;
```

51.Sales Person

Question: Write a SQL query to report the names of all the salespersons who did not have any sales orders in the given year.

```
SalesPerson (sales_id, name, salary, commission_rate, hire_date)
Orders (order_id, order_date, com_id, salesperson_id, amount)
Company (com_id, name, city)
```

Solution:

```
SELECT
    s.name
FROM
    SalesPerson s
WHERE
    s.sales_id NOT IN (
        SELECT
            salesperson_id
        FROM
            Orders
        WHERE
            YEAR(order_date) = 2019
    );
```

52.Find Customer Referee

Question: Write a SQL query to report the names of the customer that are not referred by the customer with id = 2.

Customer (id, name, referee_id)

Solution:

```sql
SELECT
    name
FROM
    Customer
WHERE
    referee_id != 2
    OR referee_id IS NULL;
```

53. Customer Who Visited but Did Not Make Any Transactions

Question: Write a SQL query to find the customers who visited the mall but did not make any transactions.

```
Visits (visit_id, customer_id)
Transactions (transaction_id, visit_id, amount)
```

Solution:

```sql
SELECT
    v.customer_id
FROM
    Visits v
LEFT JOIN
    Transactions t ON v.visit_id = t.visit_id
WHERE
    t.transaction_id IS NULL
GROUP BY
    v.customer_id;
```

54.Second Highest Salary

Question: Write a SQL query to get the second highest salary from the `Employee` table.

Employee (id, salary)

Solution:

```sql
SELECT
  MAX(salary) AS SecondHighestSalary
FROM
  Employee
WHERE
  salary < (
    SELECT
      MAX(salary)
    FROM
      Employee
  );
```

55.Percentage of Repeated Players

Question: Write an SQL query to find the percentage of players that logged in more than once in the given period.

Activity (player_id, device_id, event_date, games_played)

Solution:

```
SELECT
  ROUND(
    COUNT(DISTINCT CASE WHEN COUNT(player_id) > 1 THEN
player_id END) * 100.0
    / COUNT(DISTINCT player_id),
    2
  ) AS percentage
FROM
  (SELECT
    player_id,
    COUNT(*) AS login_count
  FROM
    Activity
  GROUP BY
    player_id) t;
```

56.Total Sales Amount by Year

Question: Write an SQL query to find the total sales amount of each year.

Product (product_id, product_name, unit_price)

Sales (seller_id, product_id, buyer_id, sale_date, quantity, price)

Solution:

```sql
SELECT
    YEAR(sale_date) AS year,
    SUM(price * quantity) AS total_sales
FROM
    Sales
JOIN
    Product ON Sales.product_id = Product.product_id
GROUP BY
    year;
```

57.User Purchase Platform

Question: Write an SQL query to get the names of the users who made purchases on both the "desktop" and "mobile" platforms.

Users (user_id, name)

Purchases (purchase_id, user_id, platform)

Solution:

```sql
SELECT
    u.name
FROM
    Users u
JOIN
    Purchases p1 ON u.user_id = p1.user_id
JOIN
    Purchases p2 ON u.user_id = p2.user_id
WHERE
    p1.platform = 'desktop'
    AND p2.platform = 'mobile'
GROUP BY
    u.name;
```

58.Product Price at a Given Date

Question: Write an SQL query to get the price of each product on a given date.

Products (product_id, new_price, change_date)

Solution:

```sql
SELECT
    product_id,
    (SELECT
        new_price
    FROM
        Products p2
    WHERE
        p1.product_id = p2.product_id
        AND p2.change_date <= '2019-08-16'
    ORDER BY
        p2.change_date DESC
    LIMIT 1) AS price
FROM
    Products p1
GROUP BY
    product_id;
```

59.Task Scheduler

Question: Write an SQL query to find the maximum number of tasks that can be completed by a single worker on a given day.

Tasks (task_id, worker_id, start_date, end_date, complete)

Solution:

```
SELECT
    worker_id,
    MAX(task_count) AS max_tasks
FROM
    (SELECT
        worker_id,
        COUNT(*) AS task_count
    FROM
        Tasks
    WHERE
        complete = 1
        AND end_date = '2023-05-01'
    GROUP BY
        worker_id) t
GROUP BY
    worker_id;
```

60. Biggest Single Number

Question: Write an SQL query to find the largest number in the MyNumbers table.

MyNumbers (num)

Solution:

```sql
SELECT
    MAX(num) AS biggest_num
FROM
    MyNumbers;
```

61.Customers Who Never Order

Question: Write a SQL query to find all customers who never ordered anything.

```
Customers (id, name)
Orders (id, customer_id)
```

Solution:

```sql
SELECT
    c.name AS 'Customers'
FROM
    Customers c
WHERE
    c.id NOT IN (
      SELECT
          customer_id
      FROM
          Orders
    );
```

62.Investments in 2016

Question: Write a SQL query to find the sum of all investments made in 2016.

Investments (investment_id, investor_id, amount, date)

Solution:

```sql
SELECT
    SUM(amount) AS total_investment
FROM
    Investments
WHERE
    YEAR(date) = 2016;
```

63.Swap Salary

Question: Write a SQL query to swap the salaries of employees with Reid and Sanders.

Salary (id, name, sex, salary)

Solution:

```
UPDATE
  Salary
SET
  salary = (
    CASE WHEN name = 'Reid' THEN (
        SELECT salary
        FROM Salary
        WHERE name = 'Sanders'
    )
    WHEN name = 'Sanders' THEN (
        SELECT salary
        FROM Salary
        WHERE
            name = 'Reid'
    )
    ELSE salary
  END
);
```